The Hebrew People of the Bible

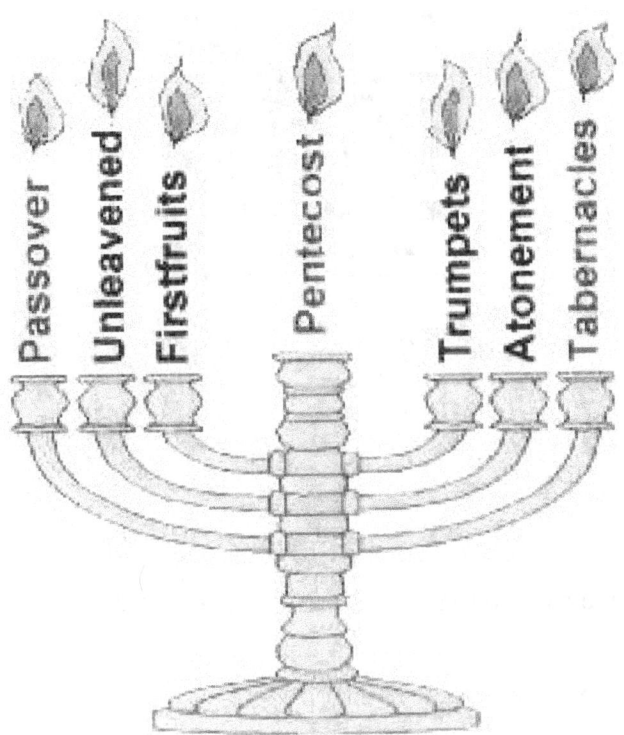

Old Testament

By Karajah Yashar

Orlando, FL 2024

www.bspbooks.com

The Hebrew People of the Bible: THE OLD TESTAMENT

All illustrations have been generated by ChatOn and DaVinci artificial intelligence language models. All stories have been produced with ChatGPT.

ISBN: 978-1-962691-21-5

First Edition: April 2024

Table of Contents

The Hebrew Story.......4

Adam and Eve..........6

Cain and Able...........9

Noah....................12

Shem................... 15

Enoch...................18

Abraham................21

Sarah...................25

Isaac....................28

Revekah.................31

Jacob...................34

Rachel..................37

Joseph..................40

Moses...................44

Aaron...................48

Joshua..................51

Sampson................54

Naomi...................57

Deborah.................60

Samuel..................63

Eli.......................66

King Saul...............69

Hannah..................72

King David..............75

Bathsheba..............79

King Solomon...........82

King Rehoboam........85

Queen Esther..........88

Job.....................91

Isaiah...................94

Jeremiah................97

Daniel..................100

King Ahab..............103

Elijah...................105

Queen Athaliah........108

The Hebrew Story

The Hebrew people, also known as the Israelites, play a central role in the biblical narrative. Their story begins with Adam and Even with a bloodline that carries on to the patriarch Abraham, whom God chooses to be the father of a great nation. Through Abraham's descendants, Isaac and Jacob, the Hebrew people are established as a distinct ethnic and religious group with a unique covenantal relationship with God.

The Hebrew people's journey is marked by several key events and themes that shape their identity and destiny. One of the defining moments in their history is the Exodus from Egypt, led by Moses. Under the oppressive rule of Pharaoh, the Hebrews are enslaved and subjected to harsh labor. However, God hears their cries and sends Moses to deliver them from bondage. Through a series of miraculous plagues and the parting of the Red Sea, the Hebrew people are liberated from Egypt and begin their journey towards the Promised Land.

During their forty years of wandering in the wilderness, the Hebrew people receive the Ten Commandments and other laws from God, establishing the foundation of their religious and moral code. Despite facing challenges and hardships, including hunger, thirst, and internal strife, the Hebrews continue to journey towards the land of Canaan, which God has promised to give them as an inheritance.

Upon entering the Promised Land, the Hebrew people face opposition from the indigenous Canaanite tribes, whom they must conquer and dispossess in order to establish their own nation. Under the leadership of figures such as Joshua, the Hebrews wage military campaigns to secure their territory and establish themselves as a sovereign nation under God's rule.

Throughout their history, the Hebrew people experience periods of prosperity and peace, as well as times of hardship and exile. They establish a monarchy under kings such as Saul, David, and Solomon, building the Temple in Jerusalem as a center of worship and religious observance. However, their kingdom is eventually divided into the northern kingdom of Israel and the southern kingdom of Judah, which are both eventually conquered by foreign powers such as the Assyrians and Babylonians.

The Hebrew people's experience of exile and dispersion becomes a central theme in their identity and religious consciousness. Following the destruction of the Temple in Jerusalem and the Babylonian exile, the Hebrew people undergo a period of spiritual and cultural renewal, eventually returning to the land of Israel and rebuilding their community.

Throughout their long and tumultuous history, the Hebrew people remain bound by their covenantal relationship with God, which is characterized by obedience, faithfulness, and a commitment to the ethical and moral principles outlined in the Torah. Their story serves as a testament to the enduring power of faith, resilience, and the belief in God's promise of redemption and restoration.

Adam and Eve

Adam and Eve, the first people from the Book of Genesis in the Bible, have captivated the imagination of believers and scholars alike for millennia. Their story, rooted in the creation of heaven and earth, is rich with symbolism and moral lessons that continue to resonate with readers across cultures and generations. As the first humans created by God, Adam and Eve's tale is foundational to Israelite theology and has left an indelible mark on the world.

The story of Adam and Eve begins in the Garden of Eden, a paradise where they lived in harmony with God and nature. They enjoyed unfettered access to all the blessings of creation, except for one prohibition: they were forbidden to eat the fruit from the Tree of the Knowledge of Good and Evil. This simple commandment, however, became the focal point of their moral journey and the catalyst for their fall from grace.

The serpent, which is a parasite (the most subtle of all creatures) is a symbol of temptation or evil and cunningly convinced Eve to eat from the forbidden tree, promising her that she would become like God. Eve, seduced by the allure of knowledge and power, succumbed to temptation and ate the fruit. She then offered it to Adam, who also partook, thereby disobeying the divine commandment. In that moment, their innocence was lost, and they became aware of their nakedness and the consequences of their actions.

Lessons:

The story of Adam and Eve teaches several profound lessons that remain relevant today. One of the most fundamental is the nature of free will and its consequences. Despite being created in the image of God and living in paradise, Adam and Eve had the freedom to choose between obedience and disobedience. Their decision to disobey God's command led to their expulsion from Eden and introduced sin and suffering into the world. This highlights the moral responsibility that comes with free will and the importance of making wise choices.

Another lesson from the story of Adam and Eve is the peril of succumbing to temptation. The serpent's subtle manipulation of Eve demonstrates how temptation often presents itself in attractive and deceptive ways, luring individuals away from what is right and good. Eve's decision to prioritize her desires over God's command serves as a cautionary tale about the dangers of selfishness and the need for discernment in the face of temptation.

Furthermore, Adam and Eve's fall from grace underscores the consequences of disobedience and the importance of accountability. Despite Adam's attempt to shift blame onto Eve and ultimately onto God Himself, they both faced the repercussions of their actions. This emphasizes the principle that actions have consequences and that individuals must take responsibility for their choices, even when tempted to shirk accountability.

Moreover, the story of Adam and Eve highlights the complexities of human nature, including vulnerability, curiosity, and the quest for knowledge. While their disobedience resulted in their expulsion from Eden, it also marked the beginning of their journey towards self-awareness and moral growth. In this sense, their story is not only one of loss and punishment but also of redemption and the possibility of spiritual renewal.

Cain and Abel

The story of Cain and Abel found in the Book of Genesis, offers profound insights into human nature, sibling dynamics, and the consequences of envy and resentment. As one of the earliest narratives in the Bible, it continues to captivate readers with its timeless themes and moral lessons.

Cain and Abel were the sons of Adam and Eve, born after their expulsion from the Garden of Eden. The story begins with Cain and Abel both offering sacrifices to God: Abel, a shepherd, offered the finest of his flock, while Cain, a farmer, offered some of his crops. God favored Abel's offering but rejected Cain's, leading to Cain's jealousy and anger towards his brother.

The central event of the story occurs when Cain lures Abel into a field and kills him out of envy and resentment. When God confronts Cain about Abel's whereabouts, Cain famously responds with the question, "Am I my brother's keeper?" This callous response not only denies responsibility but also reveals Cain's disregard for the sanctity of life and his own moral culpability.

Lessons:

The story of Cain and Abel offers several important lessons that remain relevant today. One of the primary lessons is the destructive power of jealousy and envy. Cain's jealousy towards Abel stems from God's favoritism towards his brother's sacrifice. This jealousy festers into resentment, ultimately leading Cain to commit the heinous act of fratricide. The story serves as a cautionary tale about the corrosive effects of envy, which can poison relationships and lead to tragic outcomes if left unchecked.

Furthermore, the story highlights the importance of personal responsibility and accountability. Despite Cain's attempt to evade responsibility for his actions, God holds him accountable for the murder of his brother. This underscores the biblical principle that individuals are responsible for their choices and actions, and they cannot absolve themselves of guilt by shifting blame onto others.

Moreover, the story of Cain and Abel emphasizes the value of righteousness and obedience to God. Abel's sacrifice is accepted because it is offered with a sincere heart and a spirit of obedience, whereas Cain's sacrifice is rejected because it lacks the same level of devotion. This highlights the importance of integrity and sincerity in one's relationship with God and serves as a reminder that true worship requires more than just outward rituals—it requires a genuine commitment of the heart.

Additionally, the story of Cain and Abel sheds light on the complexities of sibling relationships and the potential for rivalry and conflict. While siblings can share a deep bond, they are also susceptible to jealousy and competition, particularly when comparisons are made or favoritism is perceived. Cain's jealousy towards Abel serves as a stark reminder of the dangers of sibling rivalry and the need for love, compassion, and mutual respect within families.

Noah

Noah, depicted in the Book of Genesis, stands as a symbol of faith, righteousness, and obedience in the face of adversity. His story, immortalized in the narrative of the Great Flood, serves as a powerful testament to the enduring power of God's mercy and the importance of moral integrity amidst a world engulfed in corruption and wickedness.

Noah lived in a time when humanity had become exceedingly wicked and corrupt. God, grieved by the wickedness of humanity, decides to bring judgment upon the earth by flooding it and destroying all living creatures, except for Noah and his family. Noah is described as a righteous man who walked faithfully with God amidst a corrupt and depraved society.

In Genesis 6:9, it is written: "Noah was a righteous man, blameless among the people of his time, and he walked faithfully with God." This verse highlights Noah's righteousness and faithfulness to God, which set him apart from the sinful world around him. Because of his righteousness, God chooses Noah to be the instrument through which He will preserve a remnant of humanity and the animal kingdom.

God instructs Noah to build an ark, a massive vessel that will serve as a refuge from the coming floodwaters. Despite the incredulity of others and the immense scale of the task, Noah obeys God's command and diligently constructs the ark according to God's specifications. Noah's obedience and faithfulness to God's instructions demonstrate his unwavering trust in God's promises and his commitment to carrying out God's will, even in the face of ridicule and skepticism.

After the ark is completed, Noah, along with his wife, his three sons (Shem, Ham, and Japheth), and their wives, enter the ark along with pairs of every kind of animal, as instructed by God. As the floodwaters cover the earth and destroy all living creatures, Noah and his family are safely sheltered within the ark, preserved from the destruction that befalls the rest of humanity.

After the floodwaters recede and the ark comes to rest on the mountains of Ararat, God makes a covenant with Noah, promising never again to destroy the earth by flood. As a sign of this covenant, God sets a rainbow in the sky as a reminder of His promise. Noah and his family emerge from the ark, and they offer sacrifices to God in thanksgiving for His deliverance and mercy.

Lessons:

One of the central lessons we can glean from the story of Noah is the importance of faith and obedience. Despite the seemingly insurmountable task set before him, Noah trusts in God's guidance and faithfully follows His instructions without question. His unwavering faith serves as a beacon of hope amidst the moral decay and disbelief that permeated the world at that time. Noah's example reminds us that obedience to God's will, even in the face of doubt and opposition, is the path to righteousness and salvation.

Furthermore, the story of Noah underscores the consequences of sin and the necessity of divine judgment. The flood serves as a sobering reminder of the consequences of human wickedness and the imperative of moral accountability. God's decision to spare Noah and his family while bringing judgment upon the rest of humanity highlights the biblical principle that righteousness and obedience to God's commands are rewarded, while sin and disobedience lead to destruction.

Another lesson we can draw from the story of Noah is the importance of perseverance and steadfastness in the face of adversity. Building the ark was undoubtedly a monumental task that required years of labor and dedication. Despite facing numerous challenges and obstacles, including mockery and scorn from his neighbors, Noah remained steadfast in his commitment to fulfilling God's will. His perseverance serves as a testament to the power of determination and resilience in overcoming obstacles and fulfilling God's purpose for our lives.

Moreover, the story of Noah emphasizes the significance of God's covenant and promise. Following the flood, God establishes a covenant with Noah and his descendants, promising never again to destroy the earth with a flood and providing the rainbow as a sign of this covenant. This covenant serves as a demonstration of God's mercy and grace, offering humanity a second chance and a renewed opportunity for redemption.

Through Noah's unwavering faith, obedience, perseverance, and God's covenant, we learn valuable lessons about the importance of righteousness, moral accountability, and the enduring power of God's mercy. Noah's story challenges us to emulate his example of faithfulness and obedience, even in the face of adversity, and reminds us of the transformative power of God's love and grace in our lives.

Shem

Shem plays a prominent role in the Book of Genesis and is often regarded as one of the patriarchs of the Israelite nation. As the eldest son of Noah, Shem is a pivotal character in the narrative of the great flood and the subsequent repopulation of the earth. His life story offers valuable lessons in faith, obedience, and the preservation of God's covenant.

Shem's story begins with his involvement in the monumental event of the great flood, where he, along with his father Noah, his mother, and his brothers, is chosen by God to survive the deluge that engulfs the earth. As one of the eight individuals aboard the ark, Shem witnesses firsthand the devastation wrought by the floodwaters and the miraculous preservation of life through God's providence.

Lessons:

One of the primary lessons we can learn from Shem's life is the importance of faithfulness and obedience to God's commands. Despite the enormity of the task entrusted to him and his family, Shem remains steadfast in his commitment to follow God's instructions and carry out His will. His obedience to God's command to enter the ark and his faithfulness in preserving the animals entrusted to his care serve as a model for believers, encouraging them to trust in God's promises and to obey His commands, even in the face of uncertainty and adversity.

Furthermore, Shem's story highlights the theme of divine providence and the preservation of God's covenant through successive generations. After the floodwaters recede and the ark comes to rest on the mountains of Ararat, God makes a covenant with Noah and his sons, including Shem, promising never again to destroy the earth by flood. As a sign of this covenant, God sets a rainbow in the sky as a reminder of His promise. Shem's participation in this covenant underscores the importance of preserving God's covenant and passing it on to future generations.

Additionally, Shem's story teaches us about the significance of family and heritage in shaping our identity and destiny. As the ancestor of the Semitic peoples, including the Israelites and the Arabs, Shem's lineage has far-reaching implications for the course of human history. His descendants play a crucial role in the biblical narrative, and their actions and decisions shape the destiny of nations. Shem's story emphasizes the importance of honoring our familial heritage and preserving the legacy of faith passed down to us by our ancestors.

Moreover, Shem's story serves as a reminder of the enduring nature of God's promises and the importance of trusting in His providence. Despite the challenges and uncertainties of life, Shem remains confident in God's faithfulness and His ability to fulfill His promises. His story encourages believers to trust in God's promises, even in the midst of adversity, knowing that He is faithful to His word and His covenant.

In conclusion, Shem's life offers valuable lessons in faith, obedience, and the preservation of God's covenant. Through his unwavering commitment to following God's commands, his participation in God's covenant, and his trust in God's providence, Shem serves as a model for believers seeking to walk faithfully with God. His story reminds us of the importance of trusting in God's promises, preserving our heritage of faith, and passing on the legacy of faithfulness to future generations.

Enoch

Enoch, while relatively lesser-known compared to other prominent characters like Noah or Moses, offers valuable lessons and inspiration through his remarkable life and legacy. Enoch's story, found in the Book of Genesis and expanded upon in other ancient texts, provides insights into faith, righteousness, and intimacy with God.

Enoch is introduced in Genesis as the great-grandson of Adam, the son of Jared, and the father of Methuselah. What sets Enoch apart from his contemporaries is his unique relationship with God and his extraordinary fate. The Bible states that "Enoch walked faithfully with God; then he was no more, because God took him away" (Genesis

5:24, NIV). This cryptic passage suggests that Enoch's faithfulness and intimacy with God were so profound that he was taken directly into heaven without experiencing death.

Lessons:

One of the primary lessons we can learn from the life of Enoch is the importance of faithfulness and intimacy in our relationship with God. Enoch's close communion with God, characterized by a life of obedience and devotion, serves as a model for believers seeking to cultivate a deeper spiritual connection with the divine. Enoch's faithfulness demonstrates that a life lived in close fellowship with God is not only possible but also immensely rewarding, leading to a transformed existence and ultimate communion with the divine.

Furthermore, Enoch's story challenges us to rethink our understanding of mortality and the afterlife. His unique fate of being taken directly into heaven without experiencing physical death offers hope and reassurance to believers, affirming the promise of eternal life and the possibility of transcending the limitations of the earthly realm. Enoch's example encourages us to embrace a perspective of eternity and to live with a sense of purpose and destiny beyond the confines of this present life.

Moreover, Enoch's legacy extends beyond his personal relationship with God to his role as a prophetic figure. The Book of Jude in the New Testament refers to Enoch as a prophet, quoting from an apocryphal text known as the Book of Enoch. According to this text, Enoch prophesied about the coming judgment of God and the return of the Lord with His holy ones. Enoch's prophetic ministry underscores the importance of speaking truth to power and proclaiming God's righteousness and justice in a world marred by sin and injustice.

In addition, Enoch's story highlights the transformative power of faith to transcend cultural norms and societal expectations. In the midst of a corrupt and sinful world, Enoch chose to walk faithfully with God, even when it meant swimming against the tide of prevailing attitudes and behaviors. His example challenges us to resist conformity to the values of this world and to instead prioritize our allegiance to God and His kingdom, regardless of the cost.

In conclusion, the story of Enoch offers valuable lessons and inspiration for believers seeking to deepen their faith, cultivate intimacy with God, and live with a sense of purpose and destiny. Enoch's faithfulness, intimacy with God, prophetic ministry, and transcendent fate serve as a timeless reminder of the transformative power of faith to transcend the limitations of this earthly life and to usher us into a deeper communion with the divine.

Abraham

Abraham, revered as the patriarch of the Hebrew people—stands as an iconic figure whose life embodies faith, obedience, and the divine covenant. His story, chronicled in the Book of Genesis, offers profound lessons that continue to resonate with believers across cultures and generations.

Abraham's journey begins in the land of Ur, where he lived with his father Terah, his wife Sarai (later known as Sarah), and his nephew Lot. At the age of seventy-five, Abraham receives a divine call from God to leave his homeland and travel to a land that God would show him. In response to God's command, Abraham demonstrates unwavering faith and obedience, embarking on a journey of faith into the unknown.

Throughout his journey, Abraham encounters various trials and tests of faith, including famine, conflicts with neighboring kingdoms, and the challenge of childlessness. Despite these challenges, Abraham remains faithful to God's promises, trusting in His providence and believing that He would fulfill His covenant with him. Abraham's unwavering faith earns him the title "father of faith" and sets an example for believers to trust in God's promises, even in the face of uncertainty.

One of the most significant events in Abraham's life is the covenant that God establishes with him. In Genesis 15, God promises to make Abraham's descendants as numerous as the stars in the sky and to give them the land of Canaan as an everlasting possession. This covenant is reaffirmed throughout Abraham's life, and it forms the foundation of God's relationship with the Israelites. Through Abraham's faithfulness, God establishes a special covenant relationship with him, promising to bless him and his descendants and to make him a blessing to all the nations of the earth.

Abraham's faith is further tested when God promises him a son in his old age, despite the fact that Sarah is barren. Despite their initial doubt and disbelief, Abraham and Sarah eventually conceive and bear a son, Isaac, fulfilling God's promise to Abraham. Isaac's birth is a miraculous sign of God's faithfulness and a testament to Abraham and Sarah's unwavering trust in His promises.

In addition to his faithfulness, Abraham is also known for his hospitality and righteousness. He demonstrates hospitality towards strangers, such as the three visitors who appear to him in Genesis 18, and he intercedes on behalf of the inhabitants of Sodom and Gomorrah, pleading with God to spare the righteous. Abraham's hospitality and righteousness serve as a model for believers, emphasizing the importance of kindness, compassion, and justice in our interactions with others.

Lessons:

One of the central lessons we can glean from Abraham's life is the importance of faith in God's promises. Throughout his journey, Abraham encounters numerous trials and obstacles, including famine, warfare, and the barrenness of his wife Sarah. Despite these challenges, Abraham remains steadfast in his faith, trusting in God's promise to make him a great nation and to bless all the families of the earth through him. Abraham's faith serves as a model for believers, encouraging them to trust in God's faithfulness and to persevere in the face of adversity.

Furthermore, Abraham's story underscores the significance of obedience to God's commands. When God calls Abraham to sacrifice his beloved son Isaac, Abraham's willingness to obey, even in the face of such a profound test of faith, demonstrates his unwavering commitment to God's will. While God ultimately provides a ram as a substitute sacrifice, Abraham's obedience serves as a powerful example of surrendering one's will to God's purposes, even when it requires great sacrifice.

Additionally, Abraham's life exemplifies the importance of hospitality and kindness towards others. Throughout his journeys, Abraham demonstrates hospitality towards strangers, offering them food, shelter, and companionship. This spirit of hospitality reflects Abraham's generosity and compassion, as well as his recognition of the inherent dignity and worth of every human being. Abraham's example challenges believers to extend hospitality and kindness to others, embodying the principles of love and compassion taught by God.

Moreover, Abraham's story highlights the concept of divine covenant and the enduring nature of God's promises. God enters into a covenant with Abraham, promising to bless him and his descendants, to give them the land of Canaan as an inheritance, and to make them a great nation. This covenant establishes a special relationship between God and Abraham's descendants, emphasizing the importance of fidelity and trust in God's promises.

In conclusion, the story of Abraham offers profound lessons in faith, obedience, hospitality, and divine covenant. Abraham's unwavering faith, obedience to God's commands, hospitality towards others, and trust in God's promises serve as timeless examples for believers seeking to live lives of purpose, integrity, and devotion. By emulating Abraham's example, believers can deepen their relationship with God, cultivate virtues of faithfulness and compassion, and fulfill their calling to be agents of blessing and reconciliation in the world.

Sarah

Sarah, the wife of Abraham, is a significant figure in the Bible whose story offers valuable insights into faith, patience, and the complexities of human relationships. Despite facing challenges such as infertility, doubt, and jealousy, Sarah's journey ultimately teaches lessons of resilience, trust in God's promises, and the importance of perseverance in the face of adversity.

Sarah's story begins with her journey alongside her husband Abraham (originally named Abram) as they leave their homeland of Ur to follow God's call to a new land. As they embark on this journey of faith, Sarah's role as Abraham's wife becomes central to the unfolding narrative of God's covenant with Abraham and the promise of descendants as numerous as the stars in the sky.

Lessons:

One of the primary lessons we can glean from Sarah's life is the importance of patience and trust in God's timing. Despite facing years of infertility and the societal pressure to bear children, Sarah remains faithful to God's promise of offspring, even as she grows older. Her journey teaches believers the value of waiting on God's timing, even when circumstances seem bleak and hopeless. Sarah's eventual conception and birth of Isaac serve as a testament to God's faithfulness and the fulfillment of His promises, reminding believers that God's timing is perfect and that He is faithful to His word.

Furthermore, Sarah's story highlights the dangers of doubt and the consequences of taking matters into one's own hands. When faced with the apparent impossibility of conceiving a child in her old age, Sarah succumbs to doubt and skepticism, suggesting that Abraham conceive a child with her maidservant, Hagar. This decision leads to tension, jealousy, and ultimately, conflict within their household. Sarah's experience serves as a cautionary tale about the pitfalls of doubt and impatience, reminding believers of the importance of trusting in God's plans and refraining from taking shortcuts or compromising their integrity in pursuit of their desires.

Additionally, Sarah's story underscores the significance of forgiveness and reconciliation in relationships. Despite her initial jealousy and resentment towards Hagar and Ishmael, Sarah eventually demonstrates compassion and forgiveness towards them, acknowledging their shared humanity and recognizing God's provision for them. Sarah's journey teaches believers the importance of extending grace and forgiveness to others, even in the midst of hurt and betrayal, and the transformative power of reconciliation in healing broken relationships.

Moreover, Sarah's story serves as a reminder of the power of prayer and intercession. Despite her initial doubt and skepticism, Sarah's prayers are ultimately answered, and she conceives a child in her old age. Her story encourages believers to persist in prayer, trusting that

God hears and responds to the cries of His people and that nothing is impossible for Him.

In conclusion, Sarah's journey from doubt and infertility to faith and motherhood offers valuable lessons in patience, trust, forgiveness, and the power of prayer. Her story serves as a testament to God's faithfulness, the importance of persevering in faith, and the transformative power of His grace in the lives of His people. By emulating Sarah's example, believers can deepen their trust in God's promises, cultivate virtues of patience and forgiveness, and experience the fulfillment of His plans and purposes in their lives.

Isaac

Isaac, the son of Abraham and Sarah, is a significant figure in the Bible whose life story offers profound lessons in faith, obedience, and divine providence. Born to elderly parents who had longed for a child, Isaac's arrival was nothing short of miraculous, fulfilling God's promise to Abraham and Sarah. Through Isaac's journey, we glean insights into the complexities of human relationships, the importance of faithfulness to God's commands, and the enduring nature of divine promises.

Isaac's story begins with his birth, which is foretold by God to Abraham and Sarah despite their advanced age. Isaac's very existence serves as a testament to God's faithfulness and the fulfillment of His promises, underscoring the importance of trusting in God's timing and providence. From his birth, Isaac is set apart as a chosen vessel through whom God's covenant with Abraham will be fulfilled.

Lessons:

One of the primary lessons we can learn from Isaac's life is the importance of obedience and submission to God's will. Isaac's willingness to trust his father Abraham and submit to being bound and placed upon the altar as a sacrifice demonstrates his unwavering faith and obedience to God's command, even in the face of uncertainty and danger. Isaac's obedience serves as a model for believers, encouraging them to trust in God's wisdom and providence, even when circumstances seem dire.

Furthermore, Isaac's story highlights the importance of parental guidance and mentorship in shaping the character and destiny of future generations. Isaac's relationship with his father Abraham serves as a model of faithfulness and obedience, as he follows in his father's footsteps and continues the legacy of faith established by Abraham. Through his father's guidance and example, Isaac learns valuable lessons about trust, obedience, and devotion to God, laying the foundation for his own spiritual journey.

Additionally, Isaac's life teaches us about the power of prayer and divine intervention in times of need. When Isaac's wife Rebekah struggles with infertility, Isaac fervently prays to God for her, and she conceives twins, Jacob and Esau. This miraculous answer to prayer underscores the importance of seeking God's guidance and provision in all aspects of life, trusting that He hears and responds to the cries of His people.

Moreover, Isaac's story serves as a reminder of the enduring nature of God's promises and the importance of faithfulness to His covenant. Despite facing challenges and setbacks, Isaac remains faithful to God's covenant with Abraham, trusting in His promises and experiencing His provision and blessing throughout his life. Isaac's story encourages believers to remain steadfast in their faith, trusting that God will fulfill His promises in His perfect timing and according to His sovereign plan.

In conclusion, Isaac's life offers valuable lessons in faith, obedience, and divine providence. Through his unwavering trust in God's promises, his obedience to His commands, and his reliance on prayer and divine intervention, Isaac exemplifies the qualities of a faithful servant of God. His story serves as a timeless reminder of the importance of trusting in God's providence, remaining obedient to His will, and believing in the fulfillment of His promises, even in the face of uncertainty and adversity.

Rebekah

Rebekah is the wife of Isaac and the mother of Jacob and Esau. Rebecca's story offers valuable lessons in faith, discernment, and the providence of God.

Rebecca's story begins with her providential encounter with Abraham's servant, who is sent to find a wife for Isaac from among Abraham's relatives. As the servant prays for guidance at a well, Rebecca appears and offers him and his camels water, demonstrating her kindness, generosity, and hospitality. This act of service leads the servant to recognize Rebecca as the chosen bride for Isaac, affirming God's providential hand in orchestrating their meeting.

Lessons:

One of the primary lessons we can learn from Rebecca's life is the importance of discerning God's will and following His guidance. Despite the cultural norms and expectations of her time, Rebecca demonstrates discernment and faith in agreeing to marry Isaac and leave her homeland to join him in Canaan. Her willingness to trust in God's leading and step out in faith serves as a model for believers, encouraging them to seek God's will in their own lives and trust in His providence, even when the path ahead seems uncertain.

Furthermore, Rebecca's story highlights the importance of familial relationships and the role of parents in shaping the destiny of their children. As the mother of Jacob and Esau, Rebecca plays a pivotal role in their lives, offering guidance, support, and encouragement. However, Rebecca's favoritism towards Jacob and her manipulation of Isaac to secure the blessing for him over Esau also serve as cautionary examples of the dangers of partiality and deception within families. Rebecca's story underscores the importance of parental guidance and mentorship, as well as the need for integrity and fairness in familial relationships.

Additionally, Rebecca's story teaches us about the consequences of deception and the importance of honesty and integrity in our interactions with others. Rebecca's role in Jacob's deception of Isaac to obtain the blessing intended for Esau illustrates the far-reaching consequences of deceit and manipulation. While Jacob ultimately receives the blessing, the deceitful means by which it is obtained lead to years of estrangement between him and Esau and sow seeds of discord within their family. Rebecca's story serves as a sobering reminder of the importance of honesty, transparency, and integrity in all of our dealings, as well as the eventual consequences of deceit and manipulation.

Moreover, Rebecca's story underscores the theme of divine providence and the fulfillment of God's promises. Despite the challenges and conflicts within her family, God's plan and purpose ultimately prevail, leading to the fulfillment of His covenant with Abraham and the establishment of the nation of Israel. Rebecca's story encourages believers to trust in God's providence, even in the midst of uncertainty and adversity, knowing that He is sovereign over all things and works all things together for the good of those who love Him.

In conclusion, Rebecca's story offers valuable lessons in faith, discernment, integrity, and divine providence. Through her example, believers are encouraged to seek God's will, trust in His guidance, and live lives of honesty, integrity, and faithfulness. Rebecca's story serves as a timeless reminder of the importance of discerning God's will, following His guidance, and trusting in His providence, even in the face of uncertainty and adversity.

Jacob

Jacob, the son of Isaac and Rebekah, is a central figure in the Hebrew narrative, particularly in the Book of Genesis. His story is one of transformation, redemption, and the enduring faithfulness of God. Through Jacob's journey, we glean profound lessons in perseverance, integrity, and the transformative power of divine grace.

Jacob's story begins with his birth, marked by his grasping the heel of his twin brother Esau as they emerge from the womb. From an early age, Jacob's life is characterized by rivalry and conflict with his brother, as well as with other family members. Despite being the younger twin, Jacob is cunning and resourceful, traits that eventually earn him the birthright and blessing intended for his brother Esau.

Lessons:

One of the primary lessons we can learn from Jacob's life is the importance of perseverance and determination in the pursuit of God's promises. Despite facing numerous challenges and setbacks, including familial strife, deception, and exile, Jacob remains steadfast in his commitment to God's covenant and the promise of blessings passed down from his forefathers. His determination serves as a model for believers, encouraging them to persevere in faith and trust in God's faithfulness, even in the midst of trials and tribulations.

Furthermore, Jacob's story highlights the consequences of deceit and manipulation in human relationships. Throughout his life, Jacob resorts to deception and trickery to achieve his goals, including deceiving his father Isaac to obtain the blessing intended for Esau and tricking his uncle Laban to secure Rachel's hand in marriage. While Jacob's cunning tactics may have yielded temporary gains, they also sow seeds of discord and mistrust within his family, leading to years of conflict and estrangement. Jacob's story serves as a cautionary tale about the dangers of deceit and manipulation, emphasizing the importance of honesty, integrity, and transparency in our interactions with others.

Additionally, Jacob's story underscores the theme of divine providence and the transformative power of grace. Despite Jacob's flaws and shortcomings, God continues to work in and through his life, ultimately transforming him into a man of faith and character. Jacob's encounter with God at Peniel, where he wrestles with a mysterious figure until daybreak, symbolizes his spiritual transformation and the renewal of his identity as Israel, meaning "one who struggles with God." Through this encounter, Jacob learns humility, dependence on God, and the importance of surrendering to His will. Jacob's story serves as a testament to the grace of God, which can redeem even the most flawed and broken individuals and transform them into vessels of His glory.

Moreover, Jacob's story teaches us about the importance of reconciliation and forgiveness in restoring broken relationships. Despite the years of animosity and estrangement between Jacob and Esau, their eventual reunion is marked by reconciliation and forgiveness. Jacob's humility and contrition, as well as Esau's generosity and forgiveness, pave the way for healing and restoration within their family. Jacob's story serves as a powerful reminder of the transformative power of reconciliation and forgiveness, and the importance of extending grace and mercy to others, even in the face of past hurts and grievances.

In conclusion, Jacob's story offers profound lessons in perseverance, integrity, grace, and reconciliation. Through his journey, we learn the importance of persevering in faith, resisting the temptation of deceit and manipulation, surrendering to God's will, and extending forgiveness and grace to others. Jacob's story serves as a timeless reminder of the transformative power of divine grace to redeem and restore even the most broken and flawed individuals, and to bring healing and reconciliation to fractured relationships.

Rachel

Rachel is known for her beauty, her love story with Jacob, and her struggles with infertility. Her life story offers valuable insights into themes of love, longing, and resilience, as well as the complexities of human relationships and the sovereignty of God.

Rachel's story begins with her introduction as the younger daughter of Laban, Jacob's uncle. Despite her physical beauty, Rachel's life is marked by challenges and hardships, particularly in her relationship with her sister Leah. Rachel's love for Jacob is evident from the moment they meet, and she becomes his chosen bride. However, Laban deceives Jacob into marrying Leah first, leading to years of rivalry and tension between the two sisters.

Lessons:

One of the primary lessons we can learn from Rachel's life is the importance of patience and perseverance in the face of adversity. Despite facing years of infertility and the pain of watching her sister bear children, Rachel remains steadfast in her love for Jacob and her hope for motherhood. Her resilience in the midst of disappointment serves as a model for believers, encouraging them to trust in God's timing and to persevere in faith, even when circumstances seem bleak.

Furthermore, Rachel's story highlights the complexities of human relationships and the consequences of jealousy and rivalry. Rachel's rivalry with her sister Leah, fueled by their shared love for Jacob and the desire for children, leads to years of tension and conflict within their family. The rivalry between Rachel and Leah serves as a cautionary tale about the destructive nature of jealousy and the importance of fostering healthy and supportive relationships based on love and mutual respect.

Additionally, Rachel's story underscores the theme of divine providence and the sovereignty of God in the midst of human struggles and hardships. Despite Rachel's infertility and the challenges she faces, God ultimately hears her prayers and grants her the gift of motherhood. Rachel gives birth to Joseph, who becomes a central figure in the biblical narrative and plays a significant role in God's plan for the nation of Israel. Rachel's story serves as a testament to the faithfulness of God and His ability to bring beauty and blessing out of even the most difficult circumstances.

Moreover, Rachel's story teaches us about the importance of trusting in God's sovereignty and surrendering to His will. Despite her longing for children, Rachel ultimately surrenders her desires to God, trusting that His plan for her life is perfect and that He will fulfill His promises in His own timing. Rachel's surrender serves as a model for believers, encouraging them to trust in God's providence and to surrender their desires and struggles to Him, knowing that He is faithful to fulfill His purposes in their lives.

In conclusion, Rachel's story offers valuable lessons in patience, perseverance, trust, and surrender. Through her life journey, we learn the importance of trusting in God's timing, fostering healthy and supportive relationships, and surrendering our desires and struggles to His sovereign will. Rachel's story serves as a timeless reminder of the faithfulness of God and His ability to bring beauty and blessing out of even the most difficult circumstances.

Joseph

Joseph, is the son of Jacob and Rachel. His life story is marked by betrayal, hardship, and eventual triumph, and offers profound lessons in resilience, forgiveness, and the sovereignty of God. Through Joseph's journey, we glean insights into the power of faithfulness, the importance of integrity, and the transformative nature of forgiveness.

Joseph is described as a dreamer, receiving two significant dreams that foretell his future prominence over his family. In these dreams, his brothers' sheaves of grain bow down to his, and the sun, moon, and eleven stars (representing his family members) bow down to him. His youthful and somewhat naïve demeanor, along with his special favor in his father's eyes, provoke jealousy and animosity among his brothers.

The turning point in Joseph's life comes when his brothers, driven by jealousy, plot to kill him but instead sell him into slavery. He is taken to Egypt, where he is sold to Potiphar, an officer of Pharaoh. Despite facing trials and temptations, Joseph remains faithful to God and gains favor in Potiphar's household. However, when falsely accused by Potiphar's wife, he is thrown into prison.

Even in prison, Joseph's integrity and faithfulness shine through, and he eventually interprets the dreams of two fellow prisoners, the chief cupbearer and the chief baker. His interpretations come true, leading to the restoration of the cupbearer to his former position.

Joseph's gift of dream interpretation catches the attention of Pharaoh, who seeks his help in interpreting troubling dreams. Through God's wisdom, Joseph interprets Pharaoh's dreams as predicting seven years of abundance followed by seven years of famine. Impressed by Joseph's insight, Pharaoh appoints him as second-in-command over all of Egypt, tasked with overseeing preparations for the coming famine.

During the years of plenty, Joseph implements wise policies to store grain, ensuring Egypt's survival during the famine. When the famine affects Canaan and Joseph's family comes to Egypt seeking food, they unknowingly bow down to him, fulfilling the dreams he had as a youth.

Joseph reveals his identity to his brothers, forgives them for their past betrayal, and orchestrates the reunion of his family in Egypt. He invites his father Jacob and the rest of his family to settle in Egypt, where they prosper under his care. Before his death, Joseph assures his family that God will one day bring them back to the land of Canaan.

Lessons:

One of the primary lessons we can learn from Joseph's life is the importance of faithfulness and integrity in the face of temptation and hardship. Despite being wronged and mistreated by others, Joseph remains steadfast in his commitment to God's commands and his moral principles. His refusal to compromise his integrity, even when faced with the allure of power and revenge, serves as a model for believers, encouraging them to prioritize righteousness and faithfulness in all aspects of their lives.

Furthermore, Joseph's story highlights the theme of divine providence and the sovereignty of God in the midst of human struggles and suffering. Despite the injustices he faces, God ultimately works all things together for Joseph's good, using his experiences to fulfill His purposes and bring about redemption and reconciliation. Joseph's journey serves as a testament to the faithfulness of God and His ability to bring beauty and blessing out of even the most difficult circumstances.

Additionally, Joseph's story teaches us about the transformative power of forgiveness and reconciliation. Despite the years of separation and betrayal, Joseph forgives his brothers and extends grace and mercy to them, recognizing that God had used their actions for good. His act of forgiveness leads to reconciliation and restoration within his family, ultimately paving the way for their preservation and prosperity in Egypt. Joseph's example of forgiveness serves as a powerful reminder of the importance of extending grace and mercy to others, even in the face of past hurts and grievances.

Moreover, Joseph's story underscores the importance of humility and trust in God's timing and purposes. Despite his elevated status in Egypt, Joseph remains humble and acknowledges God's role in his success and prosperity. His humility and reliance on God's wisdom and guidance serve as a model for believers, encouraging them to trust in God's providence and to remain humble in the midst of success and prosperity.

In conclusion, Joseph's life offers valuable lessons in resilience, integrity, forgiveness, and humility. Through his journey, we learn the importance of faithfulness to God's commands, the transformative power of forgiveness and reconciliation, and the sovereignty of God in the midst of human struggles and suffering. Joseph's story serves as a timeless reminder of the faithfulness of God and His ability to work all things together for good, even in the face of adversity and injustice.

Moses

Moses, one of the most prominent figures in the Bible, is central to the narrative of the Old Testament, particularly in the Book of Exodus. His life story is rich with lessons of faith, obedience, leadership, and the transformative power of God's presence. From his humble beginnings as a Hebrew slave to his role as the great liberator and lawgiver of Israel, Moses's journey is marked by profound encounters with God and the fulfillment of His divine purposes.

Moses was born into the Hebrew tribe during a time of oppression and slavery in Egypt. Moses's mother, Jochebed, concealed him for three months after his birth to protect him from Pharaoh's decree to kill all Hebrew male infants. Eventually, she placed him in a basket and set him adrift on the Nile River, where he was found by Pharaoh's daughter and raised as an Egyptian prince in the royal household.

Despite his privileged upbringing, Moses became aware of his Hebrew heritage and felt compelled to identify with his enslaved people. In Exodus 2:11-15, Moses intervenes to defend a Hebrew slave from an Egyptian taskmaster, resulting in his flight from Egypt to the land of Midian. There, he encounters the priest of Midian, Jethro, whose daughter Zipporah he marries, and he settles into a life as a shepherd.

Moses's life takes a dramatic turn when he encounters the burning bush on Mount Horeb, where God calls him to lead the Israelites out of slavery in Egypt. In Exodus 3-4, God reveals His divine name to Moses ("I AM WHO I AM") and commissions him to confront Pharaoh and demand the release of the Hebrew slaves. Despite his initial reluctance and feelings of inadequacy, Moses ultimately obeys God's call and returns to Egypt to fulfill his mission.

The story of Moses's leadership in leading the Israelites out of Egypt is recounted in the Book of Exodus, with God performing miraculous signs and wonders to demonstrate His power and to persuade Pharaoh to let His people go. These include the ten plagues inflicted upon Egypt, culminating in the Passover, where the Israelites are spared from the final plague by the blood of the lamb.

Following their deliverance from Egypt, Moses leads the Israelites through the wilderness towards the Promised Land. During their journey, Moses receives the Ten Commandments and other laws from God on Mount Sinai, establishing the covenant between God and His people. Despite facing numerous challenges, including rebellion from the Israelites and his own personal struggles, Moses remains faithful to God's commands and serves as a mediator between God and His people.

Moses's life comes to an end on the plains of Moab, overlooking the Promised Land, where God allows him to see the land but prohibits him from entering it due to his disobedience at the waters of Meribah. In Deuteronomy 34, Moses dies at the age of 120, and God buries him in the land of Moab, though his burial place remains unknown.

Moses is remembered as a prophet, lawgiver, and leader of the Israelites, who guided them from slavery to freedom and established the foundation of their faith. His life story is celebrated for its themes of faith, obedience, liberation, and covenant, and his influence continues to shape the religious and cultural traditions of millions of people around the world.

Lessons:

One of the primary lessons we can learn from Moses's life is the importance of obedience and surrender to God's call. Despite his initial reluctance and feelings of inadequacy, Moses eventually responds to God's call to lead the Israelites out of Egypt. His obedience to God's command demonstrates his trust in God's power and sovereignty, even in the face of seemingly insurmountable obstacles.

Furthermore, Moses's story highlights the theme of God's faithfulness and provision in the midst of adversity. Throughout his journey, Moses experiences God's miraculous interventions and provision, from the parting of the Red Sea to the provision of manna in the wilderness. These miraculous signs and wonders serve as a testament to God's power and His commitment to deliver His people from bondage and lead them to freedom.

Additionally, Moses's life teaches us about the importance of perseverance and resilience in the face of opposition and hardship. Despite facing numerous challenges, including resistance from Pharaoh, grumbling from the Israelites, and his own personal struggles with doubt and frustration, Moses remains steadfast in his commitment to God's mission. His perseverance serves as a model for believers, encouraging them to trust in God's promises and to press on in faith, even when the path ahead seems difficult or uncertain.

Moreover, Moses's story underscores the importance of humility and dependence on God's strength rather than relying on our own abilities. Despite his position of leadership and authority, Moses remains humble before God, acknowledging his own limitations and weaknesses. His humility allows him to experience God's presence and guidance in a profound way, leading to intimate encounters with the divine and a deeper relationship with God.

In conclusion, Moses's life offers valuable lessons in faith, obedience, leadership, perseverance, and humility. Through his journey from a humble shepherd to the liberator and lawgiver of Israel, Moses exemplifies what it means to trust in God's promises, to obey His commands, and to walk humbly before Him. His story serves as an inspiration and a challenge to believers of all ages, reminding us of the transformative power of God's presence in our lives and the importance of surrendering to His will.

Aaron

Aaron is the older brother of Moses. He plays a central role in the narrative of the Exodus and the establishment of Israelite priesthood. Aaron's life story offers valuable lessons in leadership, faithfulness, and the consequences of compromise.

Aaron's story begins with his call to serve as a spokesperson for his brother Moses. Despite initially expressing doubt and hesitation, Aaron ultimately accepts his role and accompanies Moses on his mission to confront Pharaoh and demand the release of the Israelite slaves from Egypt. As Moses's mouthpiece, Aaron plays a crucial role in delivering God's messages and performing miraculous signs and wonders to persuade Pharaoh to let the Israelites go.

Lessons:

One of the primary lessons we can learn from Aaron's life is the importance of faithfulness and obedience to God's commands. Despite his moments of weakness and compromise, Aaron remains faithful to his calling as a servant of God and a leader of the Israelites. His willingness to obey God's instructions, even in the face of adversity and uncertainty, serves as a model for believers, encouraging them to trust in God's promises and to walk in obedience to His commands.

Furthermore, Aaron's story highlights the consequences of compromise and the dangers of idolatry. In Exodus 32, while Moses is on Mount Sinai receiving the Ten Commandments, the Israelites grow impatient and demand that Aaron make them a god to worship. Aaron, succumbing to pressure from the people, fashions a golden calf and leads the Israelites in worshiping it. This act of idolatry angers God and leads to severe consequences for the Israelites, including the destruction of the golden calf and the deaths of many who participated in the idolatrous worship.

Additionally, Aaron's story teaches us about the importance of humility and accountability in leadership. Despite his prominent position as the high priest of Israel, Aaron remains humble before God and acknowledges his own shortcomings and failures. His willingness to take responsibility for his actions and seek forgiveness from God serves as a model for leaders, reminding them of the importance of humility, integrity, and accountability in leadership.

Moreover, Aaron's story underscores the theme of God's grace and redemption. Despite his failings and shortcomings, God continues to use Aaron as His instrument and to bestow His blessings upon him and the people of Israel. Aaron's story serves as a reminder of God's faithfulness and His ability to work through imperfect vessels to accomplish His purposes.

In conclusion, Aaron's life offers valuable lessons in faithfulness, obedience, humility, and accountability. Through his story, we learn about the importance of trusting in God's promises, resisting compromise and idolatry, and walking in humility and integrity as leaders. Aaron's legacy continues to inspire and challenge believers to this day, reminding us of the importance of remaining faithful to God's commands and seeking His forgiveness and grace when we fall short.

Joshua

Joshua emerges as a central figure in the narrative of the Israelites' conquest of the Promised Land. His life story is chronicled primarily in the Book of Joshua, where he transitions from being Moses's trusted aide to becoming the leader of the Israelite nation. Joshua's journey is marked by themes of courage, faith, obedience, and the fulfillment of God's promises.

Joshua's story begins with his upbringing as a young Hebrew slave in Egypt. Despite being born into a generation marked by bondage and oppression, Joshua's faithfulness and devotion to God set him apart. He serves as Moses's assistant and witnesses firsthand the miraculous deliverance of the Israelites from slavery in Egypt, the crossing of the Red Sea, and the giving of the Law at Mount Sinai.

Lessons:

One of the primary lessons we can learn from Joshua's life is the importance of courage and faith in facing daunting challenges. When Moses dies and Joshua is appointed as his successor, he is tasked with leading the Israelites across the Jordan River into the Promised Land and conquering its inhabitants. Despite the formidable obstacles and the overwhelming nature of the task before him, Joshua remains resolute in his trust in God's promises and His presence. His unwavering courage and faith serve as a model for believers, encouraging them to trust in God's power and to step out in faith, even when the path ahead seems uncertain or intimidating.

Furthermore, Joshua's story highlights the importance of obedience to God's commands. Throughout the conquest of the Promised Land, Joshua faithfully follows the instructions given to him by God, whether it be marching around the walls of Jericho or leading the Israelites in battle against their enemies. His obedience to God's commands demonstrates his trust in God's wisdom and sovereignty and his commitment to fulfilling God's purposes for His people. Joshua's example challenges believers to obey God's commands wholeheartedly and to trust in His guidance, even when it goes against conventional wisdom or seems difficult to comprehend.

Additionally, Joshua's story teaches us about the importance of remembering God's faithfulness and the need to pass on our faith heritage to future generations. After the Israelites successfully conquer the Promised Land, Joshua instructs them to set up memorials and landmarks to commemorate God's faithfulness and to remind future generations of His mighty acts on their behalf. His emphasis on remembrance underscores the importance of preserving our spiritual heritage and passing on the stories of God's faithfulness to the next generation.

Moreover, Joshua's story underscores the theme of the sovereignty of God and His faithfulness to His promises. Throughout the conquest of the Promised Land, God demonstrates His power and faithfulness by giving the Israelites victory over their enemies and fulfilling His promise to give them the land. Joshua's story serves as a testament to God's faithfulness and His ability to fulfill His promises, even in the face of seemingly insurmountable obstacles.

In conclusion, Joshua's life offers valuable lessons in courage, faith, obedience, and remembrance. Through his unwavering trust in God's promises, his obedience to God's commands, and his commitment to passing on his faith heritage to future generations, Joshua serves as a model for believers seeking to walk faithfully with God. His story challenges us to trust in God's power, to obey His commands wholeheartedly, and to remember His faithfulness in our lives.

Sampson

Samson, a towering figure in the Hebrew nation, is known for his incredible strength, his dramatic exploits, and his tragic downfall. His story, chronicled primarily in the Book of Judges, offers valuable lessons in faithfulness, obedience, and the consequences of pride and compromise.

Samson's story begins with his miraculous birth to a barren woman named Manoah and her husband, who received a divine visitation from an angel of the Lord. The angel foretold Samson's birth and instructed that he be set apart as a Nazirite from birth, meaning he was to abstain from wine and strong drink, avoid touching dead bodies, and never cut his hair.

As Samson grows, he becomes known for his exceptional strength, which he uses to fight against the Philistines, Israel's oppressors. He famously kills a lion with his bare hands and later defeats an entire army of Philistines using only the jawbone of a donkey. Despite his physical prowess, Samson's weakness lies in his relationships with women, particularly his ill-fated love affair with Delilah.

The story of Samson and Delilah is perhaps the most famous aspect of his narrative. Delilah, bribed by the Philistine rulers, seeks to discover the secret of Samson's strength. After repeated attempts to trick him into revealing the source of his power, Samson finally succumbs to Delilah's persistence and tells her that his strength lies in his uncut hair. While Samson sleeps, Delilah cuts his hair, and he loses his strength. The Philistines seize him, gouge out his eyes, and imprison him.

In a dramatic turn of events, Samson's hair begins to grow back while he is imprisoned, and his strength returns. During a Philistine feast held in honor of their god Dagon, Samson is brought out to entertain the guests. He asks to lean against the pillars of the temple, and with a prayer to God, he pushes against them, causing the temple to collapse, killing himself and thousands of Philistines.

Samson's story is one of triumph and tragedy, filled with feats of strength and moments of weakness. While he is celebrated as a hero of faith who delivered his people from their enemies, he also serves as a cautionary tale about the dangers of pride, disobedience, and giving in to temptation.

Lessons:

One of the primary lessons we can learn from Samson's life is the importance of obedience to God's commands. Despite his great strength and potential, Samson's downfall comes as a result of his disobedience and compromise. Throughout his life, Samson struggles with temptation and repeatedly violates his Nazirite vow, engaging in relationships with foreign women and disregarding the laws and customs of his people.

Furthermore, Samson's story highlights the consequences of pride and arrogance. Despite his many victories over the Philistines, Samson becomes increasingly self-assured and complacent, leading to his eventual capture and enslavement by the Philistines. His pride blinds him to the dangers of his situation, and he is ultimately betrayed by Delilah, a Philistine woman whom he loves, leading to his capture and imprisonment.

Additionally, Samson's story teaches us about the importance of humility and dependence on God's strength rather than relying on our own abilities. Despite his great physical strength, Samson's true source of power comes from his relationship with God. It is only when he acknowledges his dependence on God and cries out to Him for help that Samson is able to defeat his enemies and fulfill his destiny as a deliverer of Israel.

Moreover, Samson's story underscores the theme of redemption and second chances. Despite his failures and shortcomings, God continues to work through Samson to accomplish His purposes and to deliver Israel from oppression. In his final act of strength, Samson pulls down the pillars of the temple of Dagon, killing himself and thousands of Philistines in the process, thus fulfilling the prophecy of his birth and delivering Israel from their enemies.

In conclusion, Samson's life offers valuable lessons in faithfulness, obedience, humility, and the consequences of pride and compromise. Through his story, we learn about the importance of obeying God's commands, remaining humble before Him, and relying on His strength rather than our own. Samson's story serves as both a warning and an encouragement to believers, reminding us of the dangers of pride and disobedience, but also of God's faithfulness to redeem and restore those who turn to Him in repentance and faith.

Naomi

Naomi, a central figure in the biblical book of Ruth, stands as a testament to resilience, faith, and the transformative power of love amidst hardship and loss. Her story, set against the backdrop of famine and bereavement, offers timeless lessons about perseverance, redemption, and the enduring bonds of family.

Naomi's journey begins in the land of Bethlehem during a time of famine, where she migrates with her husband, Elimelech, and their two sons, Mahlon and Chilion, to the land of Moab in search of sustenance. However, tragedy strikes as Naomi loses her husband and sons, leaving her widowed and destitute in a foreign land.

Lessons:

One of the primary lessons we can learn from Naomi's story is the power of resilience and perseverance in the face of adversity. Despite experiencing unimaginable loss and grief, Naomi refuses to be defined by her circumstances and remains steadfast in her faith. She demonstrates remarkable strength and resilience as she navigates the challenges of widowhood and displacement, refusing to succumb to despair and hopelessness.

Furthermore, Naomi's story highlights the importance of community and support in times of trial and tribulation. Despite the cultural and ethnic barriers that exist between Naomi and her daughter-in-law Ruth, Naomi forms a deep bond with Ruth based on mutual love and loyalty. Together, they provide comfort and companionship to one another, offering a beacon of hope amidst the darkness of their shared sorrow.

Additionally, Naomi's story emphasizes the theme of redemption and restoration in the midst of loss and despair. Despite feeling abandoned and forsaken by God, Naomi ultimately experiences a divine reversal of fortune as she returns to Bethlehem with Ruth and witnesses God's faithfulness in providing for their needs. Through the kindness and generosity of Boaz, a distant relative, Naomi and Ruth find refuge and security, and Naomi's bitterness is replaced with joy and gratitude.

Moreover, Naomi's story teaches us about the power of love and selflessness in building and sustaining relationships. Despite facing the prospect of a solitary existence in her homeland, Naomi encourages Ruth to return to her own people and seek a new life for herself. Her selfless act of love and sacrifice demonstrates the depth of her affection for Ruth and reflects her desire for Ruth's happiness and well-being.

In conclusion, Naomi's life offers valuable lessons about resilience, faith, and the transformative power of love. Through her example, we learn about the importance of perseverance in the face of adversity, the significance of community and support in times of trial, and the possibility of redemption and restoration amidst loss and despair. Naomi's story serves as a source of inspiration and encouragement for believers, reminding us of God's faithfulness and provision in all circumstances, and the enduring power of love to overcome even the greatest of challenges.

Deborah

Deborah is celebrated as a prophetess, judge, and military leader of ancient Israel. Her story, found in the Book of Judges, offers valuable lessons in leadership, courage, and the power of faith in God.

Deborah's story begins during a tumultuous period in Israel's history, characterized by cycles of idolatry, oppression, and deliverance. As a prophetess, Deborah serves as a spiritual leader and advisor to the people, offering guidance and counsel in matters of faith and governance. She holds court under a palm tree in the hill country of Ephraim, where the Israelites come to seek her wisdom and judgment.

Lessons:

One of the primary lessons we can learn from Deborah's life is the importance of using one's gifts and abilities to serve others and advance God's purposes. Despite living in a male-dominated society, Deborah rises to prominence as a leader and demonstrates remarkable courage and conviction in her role as a judge and military strategist. Her willingness to step into positions of leadership and authority challenges societal norms and inspires others to recognize and honor the gifts and talents of women.

Furthermore, Deborah's story highlights the power of courage and faith in the face of daunting challenges and adversity. When the Israelites are oppressed by Jabin, the king of Canaan, Deborah calls upon Barak, a military commander, to lead the Israelite army into battle against their oppressors. Despite Barak's initial hesitation and fear, Deborah reassures him of God's presence and promises victory. With Deborah's guidance and encouragement, Barak leads the Israelite forces to a decisive victory over the Canaanite army, liberating the people from their oppression.

Additionally, Deborah's story emphasizes the importance of trusting in God's sovereignty and faithfulness in times of uncertainty and conflict. Deborah's faith in God's promises and her unwavering commitment to His cause enable her to lead the Israelites with wisdom, courage, and determination. Through her leadership, God demonstrates His power to deliver His people and fulfill His purposes, even in the midst of seemingly impossible circumstances.

Moreover, Deborah's story teaches us about the value of collaboration and teamwork in achieving common goals and objectives. Deborah works closely with Barak and other leaders in Israel, fostering unity and cooperation among the tribes in the face of external threats. Her ability to build consensus and inspire collective action enables the Israelites to overcome their adversaries and achieve victory.

In conclusion, Deborah's life offers timeless lessons in leadership, courage, and faithfulness. Through her example, we learn about the importance of using one's gifts and talents to serve others, the power of courage and faith in the face of adversity, and the value of collaboration and teamwork in achieving common goals. Deborah's story continues to inspire and challenge believers to rise up as courageous leaders and agents of change, trusting in God's faithfulness and provision in all circumstances.

Samuel

Samuel is prominently featured in the books of 1 Samuel and 2 Samuel. His life story is marked by themes of prophecy, leadership, and the transition from the period of the judges to the establishment of the monarchy in Israel. Samuel's journey offers valuable lessons in faithfulness, obedience, and the importance of discerning God's voice.

Samuel's story begins with his miraculous birth to Hannah, a barren woman who fervently prayed for a child. In response to her prayers, God grants her a son, whom she dedicates to the service of the Lord. Samuel grows up under the mentorship of Eli, the high priest at the tabernacle in Shiloh, where he learns to recognize and respond to the voice of God.

Lessons:

One of the primary lessons we can learn from Samuel's life is the importance of listening to and obeying God's voice. From a young age, Samuel demonstrates a sensitivity to the voice of God and a willingness to follow His instructions, even when they are difficult or challenging. In 1 Samuel 3, Samuel receives a prophetic call from God in the middle of the night, and despite his initial confusion, he responds with humility and obedience, saying, "Speak, for your servant is listening." This willingness to listen and obey sets Samuel apart as a faithful servant of God and prepares him for his role as a prophet and leader of Israel.

Furthermore, Samuel's story highlights the importance of integrity and righteousness in leadership. As a prophet and judge of Israel, Samuel serves as a moral compass for the nation, calling them to repentance and obedience to God's commands. Despite facing pressure from the people to appoint a king to rule over them, Samuel remains steadfast in his commitment to God's sovereignty and warns them of the potential consequences of having a human king. His integrity and righteousness serve as a model for leaders, reminding them of the importance of prioritizing God's will above their own desires and ambitions.

Additionally, Samuel's story teaches us about the faithfulness and sovereignty of God in fulfilling His promises. Despite the faithlessness and disobedience of the Israelites, God remains faithful to His covenant with them and raises up Samuel as a prophet and judge to guide them back to Himself. Through Samuel's leadership, God brings about renewal and revival among His people, demonstrating His power to work all things together for good, even in the midst of human failures and shortcomings.

Moreover, Samuel's story underscores the importance of humility and dependence on God's strength rather than relying on our own abilities. Despite his position of authority as a prophet and judge,

Samuel remains humble before God, acknowledging his own limitations and weaknesses. His humility allows him to hear and respond to God's voice with clarity and discernment, guiding him in his leadership and decision-making.

In conclusion, Samuel's life offers valuable lessons in faithfulness, obedience, integrity, and humility. Through his example, we learn about the importance of listening to God's voice, obeying His commands, and prioritizing His will above our own desires. Samuel's story serves as an inspiration and a challenge to believers of all ages, reminding us of the faithfulness and sovereignty of God and the importance of walking faithfully with Him.

Eli

Eli is best known for his role as a high priest and judge of Israel during a tumultuous period in the nation's history. His story, chronicled primarily in the books of 1 Samuel, offers valuable lessons in leadership, integrity, and the consequences of failing to discipline one's children.

Eli's story begins with his appointment as high priest of Israel, succeeding his mentor, the aging priest Samuel. As high priest, Eli served as the spiritual leader and mediator between the people and God, overseeing the religious practices and sacrifices at the tabernacle in Shiloh.

Lessons:

One of the primary lessons we can learn from Eli's life is the importance of integrity and obedience to God's commands. Despite his position of authority, Eli's leadership is marred by a failure to discipline his sons, Hophni and Phinehas, who serve as priests alongside him. The sons of Eli are described as corrupt and wicked, abusing their authority and dishonoring God by their immoral behavior and disregard for the sanctity of the priesthood.

Furthermore, Eli's story highlights the consequences of failing to discipline one's children and hold them accountable for their actions. Despite warnings from fellow priests and even from God Himself, Eli fails to take decisive action to restrain his sons or remove them from their positions of authority. This failure to address the wrongdoing of his sons ultimately leads to God's judgment on Eli's household and the loss of the priesthood from his descendants.

Additionally, Eli's story teaches us about the importance of humility and repentance in response to God's rebuke. When the prophet Samuel delivers a message of judgment against Eli and his family, Eli humbly accepts the rebuke and acknowledges the righteousness of God's judgment. Despite the severity of the consequences, Eli remains faithful to God and entrusts His judgment, saying, "He is the Lord; let him do what is good in his eyes."

Moreover, Eli's story underscores the theme of God's faithfulness and sovereignty in fulfilling His purposes, even in the midst of human failure and sin. Despite the corruption and disobedience of Eli's household, God remains faithful to His promises and raises up a new leader in Samuel, who serves as both prophet and judge over Israel. Through Samuel, God continues to work out His plan of redemption and deliverance for His people, demonstrating His power to bring about good even in the face of human frailty and disobedience.

In conclusion, Eli's life offers valuable lessons in leadership, integrity, and the consequences of failing to discipline one's children. Through his example, we learn about the importance of obeying God's commands, holding others accountable for their actions, and humbly accepting God's discipline and correction. Eli's story serves as a sobering reminder of the dangers of complacency and compromise in leadership, and the importance of remaining faithful to God's standards of righteousness and justice.

King Saul

King Saul, the first king of Israel, is a significant figure in the Bible, particularly in the books of 1 Samuel and 2 Samuel. His life story is a complex narrative marked by themes of leadership, obedience, pride, and the consequences of disobedience. Saul's journey from a humble farmer to the anointed king of Israel offers valuable lessons in leadership, faith, and the importance of seeking God's guidance.

Saul's story begins with his anointing as king by the prophet Samuel, in response to the people's demand for a king to rule over them. Despite his initial reluctance and feelings of inadequacy, Saul eventually accepts the mantle of kingship and leads the Israelites in battle against their enemies, particularly the Philistines. In the early years of his reign, Saul enjoys success and popularity among the people, as he leads them to victory in battle and establishes stability and security within the kingdom.

Lessons:

One of the primary lessons we can learn from Saul's life is the importance of obedience to God's commands. Despite being chosen by God as king and anointed by His prophet, Saul's reign is marked by moments of disobedience and rebellion against God's will. In 1 Samuel 15, Saul is commanded by God to completely destroy the Amalekites and all their possessions, yet he spares the king, Agag, and the best of the livestock. This act of disobedience leads to God's rejection of Saul as king and the eventual transfer of the kingship to David.

Furthermore, Saul's story highlights the dangers of pride and the consequences of allowing pride to rule over one's heart. As Saul's reign progresses, he becomes increasingly consumed by jealousy and insecurity, particularly in relation to David, who gains popularity and favor among the people. Saul's jealousy ultimately drives him to seek David's destruction and leads to a tragic end for both himself and his family.

Additionally, Saul's story teaches us about the importance of seeking God's guidance and relying on His wisdom in times of decision-making and crisis. Despite Saul's outward success as king, he fails to seek God's guidance and relies instead on his own understanding and impulses. This ultimately leads to his downfall and the loss of his kingdom. Saul's example serves as a cautionary tale for leaders, reminding them of the importance of humility and dependence on God's wisdom in their leadership.

Moreover, Saul's story underscores the theme of God's sovereignty and His ability to work all things together for good, even in the midst of human failures and shortcomings. Despite Saul's disobedience and rebellion, God remains faithful to His promises and raises up David as a king after His own heart to succeed Saul. Through David's lineage, God ultimately brings about the fulfillment of His promises to establish an eternal kingdom through the line of David's descendant, Jesus Christ.

In conclusion, Saul's life offers valuable lessons in leadership, obedience, humility, and dependence on God. Through his example, we learn about the importance of obedience to God's commands, the dangers of pride and jealousy, and the need to seek God's guidance in all aspects of life. Saul's story serves as a reminder of the consequences of disobedience and the importance of remaining faithful to God's will, even in the face of temptation and adversity.

Hannah

Hannah, a woman of faith and determination, is a prominent figure in the Bible, particularly in the books of 1 Samuel. Her story is one of prayer, perseverance, and the faithfulness of God in answering the cries of His people. Hannah's life offers valuable lessons in faith, prayer, and trust in God's providence.

Hannah's story begins with her distress over her barrenness. In a society where motherhood was highly valued, Hannah's inability to bear children brought her deep sorrow and anguish. Despite her pain, Hannah's faith in God remained steadfast. Year after year, she poured out her heart in prayer to God, fervently seeking His intervention and promising to dedicate her child to His service if He granted her the gift of motherhood.

Lessons:

One of the primary lessons we can learn from Hannah's life is the power of persistent prayer and unwavering faith in God's faithfulness. Despite facing seemingly insurmountable odds and enduring ridicule from her rival, Peninnah, Hannah continues to pray earnestly to God, trusting in His ability to hear and answer her prayers. Her perseverance in prayer serves as a model for believers, encouraging them to persist in seeking God's intervention in their lives and to trust in His timing and faithfulness.

Furthermore, Hannah's story highlights the importance of surrendering our desires and plans to God's will. In her prayer at the tabernacle in Shiloh, Hannah vows to dedicate her son to the service of the Lord if He grants her request. This act of surrender demonstrates Hannah's trust in God's wisdom and sovereignty, as she relinquishes control over her child's future and entrusts him to God's care. Her example challenges believers to surrender their hopes, dreams, and desires to God's will, trusting that His plans are ultimately for their good.

Additionally, Hannah's story teaches us about the faithfulness of God in answering the prayers of His people. In response to Hannah's heartfelt prayer, God graciously grants her the gift of motherhood, and she conceives and gives birth to a son, whom she names Samuel, meaning "heard by God." Samuel grows up to become a mighty prophet and leader in Israel, fulfilling Hannah's vow to dedicate him to God's service. Through Hannah's story, we are reminded of God's faithfulness in fulfilling His promises and His ability to bring beauty and purpose out of our deepest pain and struggles.

Moreover, Hannah's story underscores the importance of gratitude and praise in response to God's blessings. After Samuel is weaned, Hannah fulfills her vow by bringing him to the tabernacle in Shiloh to serve under the priest Eli. In her prayer of thanksgiving, known as the "Song of Hannah" (1 Samuel 2:1-10), Hannah praises God for His faithfulness, His sovereignty, and His provision. Her prayer of gratitude serves as a model for believers, reminding them of the importance of acknowledging God's blessings and giving Him thanks for His goodness and mercy.

In conclusion, Hannah's life offers valuable lessons in faith, prayer, surrender, and gratitude. Through her example, we learn about the power of persistent prayer, the importance of surrendering our desires to God's will, and the faithfulness of God in answering the cries of His people. Hannah's story serves as an inspiration and a challenge to believers of all ages, reminding us to trust in God's faithfulness, to persist in prayer, and to give thanks for His blessings.

King David

King David, a central figure in the Bible, particularly in the Old Testament, is renowned for his multifaceted character, his triumphs, and his flaws. His life story, chronicled primarily in the books of 1 Samuel through 1 Kings, is marked by themes of faith, courage, repentance, and redemption. David's journey offers valuable lessons in leadership, integrity, and the consequences of sin.

David's journey begins in humble origins, born in Bethlehem as the youngest son of Jesse, a shepherd. Despite his humble beginnings, David's destiny takes a remarkable turn when the prophet Samuel anoints him as king of Israel while he is still a young shepherd boy.

This anointing sets David on a path that ultimately leads to his becoming the second king of Israel, succeeding Saul.

David's rise to prominence is marked by numerous victories and accomplishments. As a skilled warrior and military leader, he defeats the Philistine giant Goliath, gaining widespread acclaim and earning the favor of King Saul. David's military prowess and leadership abilities further solidify his reputation, leading to his appointment as commander of Saul's army.

However, David's relationship with Saul becomes increasingly fraught as Saul grows jealous of David's popularity and success. Forced to flee for his life, David becomes a fugitive, leading a band of loyal followers and evading Saul's attempts to kill him. Despite numerous opportunities to seize the throne by force, David remains committed to God's timing and refuses to harm Saul, whom he regards as God's anointed.

After Saul's death, David ascends to the throne of Israel, ruling from the city of Jerusalem. His reign is characterized by military conquests, political alliances, and the establishment of Jerusalem as the religious and political capital of Israel. David's most notable military victory comes with the capture of Jerusalem from the Jebusites, leading to the city being known as the City of David.

David's legacy, however, extends beyond his military and political achievements. He is also renowned as a poet and musician, credited with composing many of the Psalms, which express a wide range of emotions, from joy and thanksgiving to sorrow and repentance. The Psalms, attributed to David, continue to be cherished as a source of comfort, inspiration, and worship for believers around the world.

Despite his many successes, David's reign is not without its share of challenges and moral failures. His infamous affair with Bathsheba, the wife of Uriah the Hittite, and his subsequent orchestration of Uriah's death, bring about severe consequences for David and his family. However, when confronted by the prophet Nathan, David humbly acknowledges his sin and repents before God, demonstrating his genuine remorse and desire for forgiveness.

Lessons:

One of the primary lessons we can learn from David's life is the importance of integrity and righteousness in leadership. Despite facing numerous opportunities to take matters into his own hands and seize power through unethical means, David remains committed to honoring God's commands and following His ways. Even when Saul is pursuing him and seeking to kill him, David refuses to harm Saul, acknowledging his divine appointment as king and trusting in God's timing and deliverance.

Furthermore, David's story highlights the consequences of sin and the importance of repentance and forgiveness. Despite being described as "a man after God's own heart," David is not immune to temptation and moral failure. His infamous affair with Bathsheba, the wife of Uriah the Hittite, and his subsequent attempt to cover up his sin by arranging for Uriah's death, bring about severe consequences for David and his family. However, when confronted by the prophet Nathan, David humbly confesses his sin and repents before God, demonstrating his genuine remorse and desire for forgiveness.

Additionally, David's story teaches us about the power of forgiveness and restoration in God's economy. Despite David's grievous sin, God forgives him and reaffirms His covenant with him, promising to establish his dynasty forever. David's story serves as a testament to God's grace and mercy, and His ability to redeem even the most broken and sinful individuals. Through David's experience, we learn about the importance of repentance and humility in seeking God's forgiveness and restoration.

Moreover, David's story underscores the theme of faithfulness and dependence on God's strength in times of trial and adversity. Throughout his life, David faces numerous challenges, including battles with enemies, political intrigue, and family conflicts. Yet, through it all, David remains steadfast in his faith and trust in God's promises, relying on Him for guidance, protection, and deliverance. His example encourages believers to trust in God's providence and to seek His guidance and strength in every aspect of life.

In conclusion, David's life offers valuable lessons in leadership, integrity, repentance, and faithfulness. Through his triumphs and failures, David exemplifies what it means to be a person after God's own heart, demonstrating the importance of integrity, humility, and dependence on God's strength. David's story serves as an inspiration and a challenge to believers of all ages, reminding us of the power of repentance and forgiveness, and the faithfulness of God in fulfilling His promises.

Bathsheba

Bathsheba is best known for her role in the affair with King David, which ultimately led to the birth of Solomon, one of Israel's greatest kings. Her story, chronicled primarily in the books of 2 Samuel and 1 Kings, offers valuable lessons in resilience, forgiveness, and redemption.

Bathsheba's story begins when she is introduced as the wife of Uriah the Hittite, a loyal soldier serving in King David's army. While her husband is away fighting in battle, Bathsheba is bathing on the rooftop of her house, where she catches the eye of King David. Despite being aware of Bathsheba's marital status, David succumbs to temptation and summons her to his palace, where they engage in an adulterous affair.

Lessons:

One of the primary lessons we can learn from Bathsheba's story is the importance of resilience and courage in the face of adversity. After becoming pregnant with David's child, Bathsheba finds herself in a precarious situation, as adultery was punishable by death under Israelite law. Despite the risks, Bathsheba remains steadfast and resilient, trusting in God's providence to see her through the difficult circumstances she finds herself in.

Furthermore, Bathsheba's story highlights the devastating consequences of sin and the importance of taking responsibility for one's actions. After learning of Bathsheba's pregnancy, David attempts to cover up his sin by summoning Uriah back from the battlefield and arranging for him to spend time with his wife. When this plan fails, David orders Uriah to be placed on the front lines of battle, where he is killed. Bathsheba's husband becomes a casualty of David's attempt to conceal his sin, underscoring the tragic consequences of David's actions.

Additionally, Bathsheba's story teaches us about the power of forgiveness and redemption. Despite the pain and heartache caused by David's sin, Bathsheba demonstrates a remarkable capacity for forgiveness, eventually marrying David and giving birth to Solomon, who would later become one of Israel's greatest kings. Through Bathsheba's story, we see the transformative power of God's grace to redeem even the most broken and sinful situations, offering hope and restoration to those who repent and seek forgiveness.

Moreover, Bathsheba's story underscores the importance of faithfulness and obedience to God's commands. While Bathsheba's actions may be questioned, she is portrayed sympathetically in Scripture, and her subsequent marriage to David suggests that she found favor in God's eyes. Despite the circumstances surrounding her relationship with David, Bathsheba remains faithful to God, and her story serves as a reminder of God's ability to work all things together for good, even in the midst of human frailty and sin.

In conclusion, Bathsheba's story offers valuable lessons in resilience, forgiveness, and redemption. Through her example, we learn about the importance of trusting in God's providence, taking responsibility for our actions, and seeking forgiveness and redemption when we fall short. Bathsheba's story serves as a reminder of God's grace and mercy to forgive and restore, offering hope and healing to all who repent and turn to Him in faith.

King Solomon

King Solomon, the son of King David and Bathsheba, is one of the most renowned figures in the Hebrew nation. His reign is celebrated for its wisdom, wealth, and architectural achievements, but it is also marked by moral complexities and spiritual decline. Solomon's story, chronicled primarily in the books of 1 Kings and 2 Chronicles, offers valuable lessons in wisdom, integrity, and the consequences of straying from God's path.

Solomon's story is chronicled primarily in the books of 1 Kings and 2 Chronicles. He ascended to the throne following the death of his father David and inherited a kingdom that was prosperous and relatively stable. Early in his reign, Solomon demonstrated his wisdom and discernment when he famously judged the dispute between two women claiming to be the mother of the same child, ordering the baby to be divided in two to reveal the true mother.

One of the most famous accounts of Solomon's wisdom is his encounter with God at Gibeon. In a dream, God appeared to Solomon and offered to grant him whatever he desired. Instead of asking for wealth, power, or long life, Solomon humbly requested wisdom to govern God's people with justice and righteousness. Pleased with Solomon's request, God granted him not only wisdom but also wealth and honor beyond measure.

During Solomon's reign, Israel experienced a period of unprecedented prosperity and expansion. He initiated numerous construction projects, including the building of the First Temple in Jerusalem, which became the center of Israelite worship. Solomon's wisdom and administrative skills also contributed to the establishment of a well-organized government and a thriving economy.

However, despite his early devotion to God and his wise leadership, Solomon's reign took a troubling turn as he allowed his wealth and power to lead him astray. He accumulated vast amounts of wealth through trade and taxation, built opulent palaces and temples, and entered into political alliances through marriage, including marrying foreign wives who led him into idolatry.

Solomon's departure from God's commands ultimately led to the decline of his reign and the division of the kingdom after his death. His son Rehoboam succeeded him as king, but the kingdom was soon divided into the northern kingdom of Israel and the southern kingdom of Judah.

Lessons:

One of the primary lessons we can learn from Solomon's life is the importance of seeking wisdom and discernment from God. In a dream at Gibeon, God appeared to Solomon and offered to grant him whatever he desired. Instead of asking for wealth, power, or long life,

Solomon humbly requested wisdom to govern God's people with justice and righteousness. God was pleased with Solomon's request and granted him not only wisdom but also wealth and honor beyond measure.

Furthermore, Solomon's story underscores the importance of integrity and obedience to God's commands. Despite his initial devotion to God and his wise leadership, Solomon's reign took a troubling turn as he allowed his wealth and power to lead him astray. He accumulated vast amounts of wealth through trade and taxation, built opulent palaces and temples, and entered into political alliances through marriage, including marrying foreign wives who led him into idolatry.

Additionally, Solomon's story serves as a cautionary tale about the dangers of worldly pursuits and the pursuit of pleasure apart from God. Despite his great wisdom, Solomon's heart was gradually led astray by his many wives and concubines, who worshiped foreign gods and led him into idolatry. This departure from God's commands ultimately led to the decline of Solomon's reign and the division of the kingdom after his death.

Moreover, Solomon's story highlights the fleeting nature of worldly success and the importance of prioritizing eternal values over temporary pleasures. Despite his immense wealth and power, Solomon reflects on the vanity and emptiness of his pursuits in the Book of Ecclesiastes, lamenting that all is "vanity and a striving after wind." His reflections serve as a sobering reminder of the limitations of human wisdom and the ultimate futility of life apart from God.

In conclusion, King Solomon's life offers valuable lessons in wisdom, integrity, and the dangers of straying from God's path. Through his example, we learn about the importance of seeking wisdom and discernment from God, maintaining integrity and obedience to His commands, and prioritizing eternal values over temporary pleasures. Solomon's story serves as both an inspiration and a warning, challenging us to pursue wisdom, righteousness, and faithfulness in our own lives, and to avoid the pitfalls of worldly pursuits and idolatry.

King Rehoboam

King Rehoboam, a pivotal figure in the Hebrew nation, appears in the Old Testament primarily in the books of 1 Kings and 2 Chronicles. He is known for his reign as the first king of the southern kingdom of Judah after the kingdom of Israel split into two following the death of his father, King Solomon. Rehoboam's story offers valuable lessons in leadership, humility, and the consequences of pride and arrogance.

Rehoboam's ascension to the throne of Judah came during a time of political and social upheaval. Following the death of Solomon, the northern tribes of Israel rebelled against the heavy taxation and forced labor imposed by Solomon's administration. Seeking relief from their burdens, the leaders of the northern tribes approached Rehoboam, requesting that he lighten their load.

Lessons:

One of the primary lessons we can learn from Rehoboam's story is the importance of wise and considerate leadership. When faced with the request of the northern tribes, Rehoboam sought counsel from both the older advisors who had served under his father Solomon and the younger men who had grown up with him. The older advisors counseled Rehoboam to respond favorably to the people's request, thereby earning their loyalty and goodwill. However, influenced by the younger advisors who urged him to assert his authority and maintain the oppressive policies of his father, Rehoboam chose to respond harshly to the people's plea for relief.

Furthermore, Rehoboam's story highlights the consequences of pride and arrogance in leadership. Instead of heeding the counsel of the older advisors and responding with humility and compassion, Rehoboam's pride leads him to make a decision that alienates the northern tribes and results in the division of the kingdom. His failure to listen to wise counsel and his refusal to consider the needs of his people ultimately lead to the loss of a significant portion of his kingdom and the weakening of his reign.

Additionally, Rehoboam's story teaches us about the importance of humility and repentance in response to God's discipline and correction. After the kingdom is divided and Rehoboam is left with only the tribes of Judah and Benjamin, he continues to face challenges and conflicts with neighboring nations. In the face of adversity, Rehoboam humbles himself before God and seeks His guidance and protection. Despite his earlier mistakes, Rehoboam's willingness to turn to God in humility demonstrates his growth and maturity as a leader.

Moreover, Rehoboam's story underscores the theme of God's sovereignty and faithfulness in fulfilling His purposes, even in the midst of human failure and disobedience. Despite the division of the kingdom and the challenges faced by Rehoboam and the people of

Judah, God remains faithful to His covenant with David and preserves a remnant of the tribe of Judah for the sake of His promises.

In conclusion, Rehoboam's life offers valuable lessons in leadership, humility, and the consequences of pride and arrogance. Through his example, we learn about the importance of wise and considerate leadership, the dangers of pride and arrogance, and the necessity of humility and repentance in response to God's discipline and correction. Rehoboam's story serves as a cautionary tale for leaders of all ages, reminding us of the importance of seeking wise counsel, considering the needs of others, and remaining humble before God.

Queen Esther

Queen Esther, a remarkable figure in the Old Testament, is celebrated for her bravery, wisdom, and faith in the face of adversity. Her story, chronicled in the Book of Esther, offers valuable lessons about courage, integrity, and the power of God to work through ordinary individuals to accomplish extraordinary purposes.

Queen Esther's narrative unfolds against the backdrop of ancient Persia, where she is chosen as queen by King Xerxes after a kingdom-wide search for a new queen. Raised by her cousin Mordecai, Queen Esther is initially known by her Hebrew name, Hadassah, but assumes the Persian name Esther to conceal her Hebrew identity.

Lessons:

One of the primary lessons we can learn from Queen Esther's story is the importance of courage and boldness in times of crisis. When Haman, the king's advisor, plots to annihilate the Hebrew people throughout the Persian Empire, Queen Esther faces a perilous choice: remain silent and safe, or risk her life by approaching the king to plead for the lives of her people. Despite the dangers and uncertainties she faces, Queen Esther summons the courage to act, declaring, "If I perish, I perish."

Furthermore, Queen Esther's story highlights the power of strategic planning and wisdom in navigating complex situations. Before approaching the king, Queen Esther wisely consults with Mordecai and devises a plan to invite the king and Haman to a series of banquets, where she intends to reveal Haman's wicked intentions and plead for the salvation of her people. Through her shrewdness and discernment, Queen Esther effectively exposes Haman's plot and secures the king's favor, leading to the salvation of the Hebrew people.

Additionally, Queen Esther's story emphasizes the theme of providence and divine intervention in the affairs of human history. Despite the absence of explicit references to God in the Book of Esther, His presence is evident throughout the narrative, working behind the scenes to orchestrate events and bring about deliverance for His people. Queen Esther's willingness to trust in God's providence and step out in faith serves as a powerful example for believers, reminding us of God's sovereignty and faithfulness, even in the most challenging of circumstances.

Moreover, Queen Esther's story teaches us about the importance of standing up for justice and righteousness, even in the face of opposition and persecution. Queen Esther's courage and advocacy on behalf of her people demonstrate her commitment to defending the oppressed and upholding the principles of righteousness and compassion. Her example challenges us to be bold and courageous in speaking out against injustice and oppression, and to use our voices and influence to advocate for those who are marginalized and vulnerable.

In conclusion, Queen Esther's life offers valuable lessons about courage, wisdom, and faith in the face of adversity. Through her example, we learn about the importance of standing up for what is right, trusting in God's providence, and using our gifts and talents to make a positive difference in the world. Queen Esther's story continues to inspire and challenge believers to live lives of courage, integrity, and faithfulness, trusting in God's power to work through us to accomplish His purposes.

Job

The story of Job, found in the Old Testament book bearing his name, is a profound exploration of suffering, faith, and the nature of God. Job's narrative offers valuable lessons about resilience, perseverance, and the sovereignty of God in the midst of life's trials and tribulations.

Job, described as a blameless and upright man, is suddenly thrust into a series of unimaginable hardships. In a single day, he loses his wealth, his children, and his health, leaving him destitute and in anguish. Despite his suffering, Job refuses to curse God or renounce his faith, declaring, "Naked I came from my mother's womb, and naked I will depart. The Lord gave and the Lord has taken away; may the name of the Lord be praised."

Lessons:

One of the primary lessons we can learn from Job's story is the importance of faithfulness and trust in God, even in the midst of profound suffering and loss. Despite his anguish and despair, Job remains steadfast in his faith, refusing to turn away from God or abandon his belief in His goodness and sovereignty. His unwavering trust in God's wisdom and providence serves as a powerful example for believers, reminding us of the importance of clinging to our faith in times of trial and uncertainty.

Furthermore, Job's story challenges conventional notions of divine justice and retribution. Despite being a righteous man, Job experiences intense suffering and hardship, leading him to question the fairness and justice of God's actions. Through his anguished cries and profound questioning, Job wrestles with the mysteries of human suffering and the apparent silence of God in the face of injustice. His story prompts readers to grapple with difficult questions about the nature of God and the problem of evil, ultimately pointing to the limitations of human understanding and the need for humility before the mysteries of God's ways.

Additionally, Job's story emphasizes the importance of community and support in times of suffering and adversity. Despite his friends' misguided attempts to explain his suffering as punishment for sin, Job finds solace and comfort in their presence. Through their companionship and empathy, Job is able to endure his trials with courage and resilience, highlighting the significance of community and solidarity in times of crisis.

Moreover, Job's story teaches us about the transformative power of suffering and the possibility of redemption and restoration in the midst of despair. Through his ordeal, Job experiences a profound encounter with God, leading to a deeper understanding of His majesty and sovereignty. In the end, Job is rewarded for his faithfulness and endurance, as God restores his fortunes and blesses him with greater prosperity than before.

In conclusion, Job's life offers valuable lessons about faith, suffering, and the sovereignty of God. Through his example, we learn about the importance of trust and resilience in the face of adversity, the need for humility and openness before the mysteries of God's ways, and the transformative power of suffering in shaping our character and deepening our relationship with God. Job's story continues to inspire and challenge believers to trust in God's goodness and providence, even in the darkest of times, knowing that He is always with us and working all things together for our good.

Isaiah

Isaiah, one of the major prophets of the Old Testament, stands as a towering figure whose prophetic ministry transcends time and culture. His profound insights, poetic imagery, and bold declarations of God's judgment and redemption continue to inspire believers and challenge readers to this day. Through the pages of the Book of Isaiah, readers encounter a prophet whose messages speak directly to the heart of humanity, offering valuable lessons about faith, obedience, and the character of God.

Lessons:

One of the primary lessons we can glean from Isaiah's prophetic ministry is the call to repentance and righteousness. Throughout his writings, Isaiah confronts the people of Israel with their sinfulness and rebellion against God, urging them to turn away from idolatry, injustice, and moral corruption. He reminds them of the holiness of God and the importance of living in accordance with His commands, emphasizing the need for genuine repentance and a transformation of heart.

Furthermore, Isaiah's prophecy underscores the theme of God's sovereignty and providence over human history. He declares God's power and authority over all nations and rulers, revealing His plans and purposes for the redemption and restoration of His people. Isaiah's vision of God's glory and majesty inspires awe and reverence, reminding readers of the greatness and holiness of the Almighty.

Additionally, Isaiah's prophecy contains numerous Messianic prophecies that point forward to the coming of the Messiah, Jesus Christ. He foretells the birth of a virgin-born child who will be called Immanuel, meaning "God with us." Isaiah also prophesies about the suffering and sacrificial death of the Messiah, describing Him as the "Suffering Servant" who will bear the sins of the world and bring salvation to all who believe.

Moreover, Isaiah's prophecy offers messages of comfort and hope to the people of Israel and to believers throughout history. He speaks of God's promise to restore His people, to renew His creation, and to establish His kingdom of peace and justice. Isaiah's words of encouragement and assurance provide comfort to those who are facing trials and tribulations, reminding them of God's unfailing love and His faithfulness to His promises.

In conclusion, the prophet Isaiah's ministry and writings offer valuable lessons in faith, obedience, and trust in God. Through his prophetic words, Isaiah challenges believers to remain faithful to God's commands, to trust in His sovereignty and providence, and to find hope and assurance in His promises. Isaiah's timeless message continues to inspire and guide believers today, reminding them of the faithfulness of God and His enduring love for His people.

Jeremiah

Jeremiah, often referred to as the "Weeping Prophet," occupies a prominent place in the Old Testament as a figure who embodies the complexities of prophetic ministry. His life and writings offer profound insights and valuable lessons about faith, obedience, and the relentless pursuit of God's will in the midst of adversity and opposition.

Lessons:

One of the primary lessons we can glean from Jeremiah's prophetic ministry is the importance of unwavering obedience to God's call, even in the face of daunting challenges and personal sacrifice. From his youth, Jeremiah was called by God to deliver messages of judgment and warning to the people of Judah, confronting them with their sins and calling them to repentance. Despite facing opposition, persecution, and even imprisonment, Jeremiah remained faithful to his calling, demonstrating remarkable courage and perseverance in proclaiming God's word.

Furthermore, Jeremiah's prophetic ministry underscores the theme of God's faithfulness and compassion towards His people, even in times of discipline and judgment. Despite the impending destruction of Judah and the exile of its people to Babylon, Jeremiah prophesies about God's plans to restore and redeem His people, promising a future of hope and restoration. His messages of comfort and assurance offer a ray of hope amidst the darkness of despair, reminding the people of God's unfailing love and His faithfulness to His covenant promises.

Additionally, Jeremiah's life and ministry serve as a poignant reminder of the cost of discipleship and the reality of suffering for the sake of righteousness. Throughout his prophetic career, Jeremiah endured persecution, rejection, and personal suffering as a result of his obedience to God's call. Yet, despite the hardships he faced, Jeremiah remained steadfast in his faith and continued to proclaim God's word with boldness and conviction, serving as a model of courage and resilience for believers.

Moreover, Jeremiah's prophetic ministry offers lessons about the importance of authentic worship and heartfelt devotion to God. Jeremiah denounces the superficiality of religious observance and calls the people of Judah to genuine repentance and wholehearted devotion to God. He emphasizes the importance of living lives of integrity and faithfulness, rooted in a deep relationship with God and characterized by love for Him and for others.

In conclusion, Jeremiah's life and prophetic ministry offer valuable lessons about faith, obedience, and the relentless pursuit of God's will. Through his example, we learn about the importance of unwavering obedience to God's call, the reality of suffering for the sake of righteousness, and the assurance of God's faithfulness and compassion towards His people. Jeremiah's timeless message continues to inspire and challenge believers today, reminding us of the importance of living lives of faithfulness, courage, and devotion in obedience to God's word.

Daniel

The story of Daniel, as chronicled in the Old Testament book bearing his name, is one of faith, courage, and unwavering commitment to God in the face of adversity. Through his life and experiences, Daniel offers valuable lessons about faithfulness, integrity, and the sovereignty of God over all circumstances.

Daniel was a young Hebrew man from the tribe of Judah who was taken captive to Babylon during the reign of King Nebuchadnezzar in the 6th century BCE.

Despite being exiled from his homeland, Daniel remained faithful to God and demonstrated exceptional wisdom and skill. He quickly gained favor with King Nebuchadnezzar and was appointed to high positions within the Babylonian court. Daniel's ability to interpret dreams and visions, as well as his wise counsel, earned him the respect and admiration of both kings and officials.

Throughout his life, Daniel faced numerous trials and challenges, including persecution for his faith and opposition from those who envied his success. However, he remained steadfast in his commitment to God and refused to compromise his principles. Daniel's unwavering faithfulness and dependence on God were evident in his actions, prayers, and interactions with others.

Daniel is perhaps best known for his experiences in the lion's den and the fiery furnace, both of which demonstrated God's miraculous intervention on his behalf. In the lion's den, Daniel's faithfulness to God resulted in his deliverance from certain death, as God sent an angel to shut the mouths of the lions. Similarly, in the fiery furnace, Daniel's companions Shadrach, Meshach, and Abednego were miraculously spared from harm when God intervened and protected them from the flames.

Lessons:

One of the primary lessons we can learn from Daniel's life is the importance of unwavering faith and trust in God, even in the midst of adversity and uncertainty. Throughout his life, Daniel demonstrates remarkable faithfulness and dependence on God, seeking His guidance and wisdom in all circumstances. His commitment to prayer, even in the face of opposition and persecution, serves as a powerful example for believers, reminding us of the importance of cultivating a deep and abiding relationship with God.

Furthermore, Daniel's story highlights the theme of God's sovereignty and providence over human history. Through his interpretation of dreams and visions, Daniel reveals God's plans and purposes for the nations and rulers of the world, demonstrating His power to bring about His will in the affairs of humanity. Daniel's prophecies, including those concerning the rise and fall of empires and the coming of the Messiah, serve as a testament to the faithfulness and reliability of God's word.

Additionally, Daniel's life exemplifies the importance of integrity and moral courage in the face of temptation and opposition. Despite being placed in positions of power and influence in the Babylonian court, Daniel remains true to his principles of righteousness and refuses to compromise his faith. His unwavering commitment to truth and justice earns him the respect and admiration of even his adversaries, demonstrating the transformative power of integrity and moral character.

Moreover, Daniel's story offers lessons about the importance of humility and humility in leadership. Despite his elevated status in the Babylonian court, Daniel remains humble and submissive to God's authority, recognizing that all wisdom and power come from Him alone. His willingness to acknowledge God's sovereignty and seek His guidance in all things sets him apart as a model of servant leadership, inspiring believers to follow his example in their own lives and endeavors.

In conclusion, the life and experiences of Daniel offer valuable lessons about faith, integrity, and the sovereignty of God. Through his unwavering faithfulness, steadfast commitment to righteousness, and humble dependence on God, Daniel serves as a powerful example for believers of all ages, reminding us of the importance of trusting in God's providence and living lives of faith and obedience. Daniel's timeless message continues to inspire and challenge believers today, encouraging us to stand firm in our convictions, even in the face of adversity, and to trust in God's faithfulness to guide and sustain us through all circumstances.

King Ahab

King Ahab is depicted as one of the most notorious and wicked kings of Israel. His reign, chronicled in the books of 1 and 2 Kings, serves as a cautionary tale about the dangers of disobedience, idolatry, and the consequences of leading a life contrary to God's commands.

Ahab inherited the throne of Israel from his father, King Omri, and reigned for twenty-two years alongside his infamous wife, Queen Jezebel. Together, they led the nation of Israel into a period of unprecedented spiritual and moral decline, marked by idol worship, corruption, and social injustice.

Lessons:

One of the primary lessons we can learn from the life of King Ahab is the destructive power of idolatry and disobedience to God's commands. Ahab abandoned the worship of the one true God and embraced the pagan religion of Baal, erecting altars and temples to this false deity throughout the land. His decision to forsake God's commandments and follow after idols led to divine judgment and brought calamity upon the nation of Israel.

Furthermore, King Ahab's reign highlights the influence of ungodly alliances and the dangers of compromising one's faith for the sake of political expediency. Ahab's marriage to Jezebel, a foreign princess and zealous worshiper of Baal, led to the introduction of pagan practices and beliefs into Israelite society. His willingness to accommodate Jezebel's idolatrous agenda and tolerate the persecution of God's prophets further exacerbated the spiritual decay of the nation.

Additionally, King Ahab's interactions with the prophet Elijah provide valuable lessons about the consequences of disobedience and the importance of repentance. Despite numerous warnings and confrontations with Elijah, Ahab stubbornly refused to acknowledge his sins and turn back to God. His pride and stubbornness ultimately sealed his fate, as prophesied by Elijah, and led to his demise on the battlefield.

Moreover, Ahab's story serves as a sobering reminder of the importance of leadership and the impact that rulers can have on the spiritual and moral climate of a nation. As king, Ahab wielded significant influence and authority over the people of Israel, yet he used his power for selfish and wicked purposes, leading the nation astray and bringing about its downfall.

In conclusion, the life and reign of King Ahab offer valuable lessons about the dangers of disobedience, idolatry, and moral compromise. His story serves as a warning to believers about the destructive consequences of forsaking God's commandments and following after the desires of the flesh. Ahab's legacy reminds us of the importance of remaining faithful to God's word, resisting the temptations of the world, and living lives that honor and glorify Him.

Elijah

Elijah, one of the most prominent prophets in the Old Testament, emerges as a central figure in the narrative of Israel's history. His life, chronicled primarily in the books of 1 and 2 Kings, is marked by dramatic confrontations, miraculous interventions, and unwavering faith in God. Through the story of Elijah, readers encounter profound lessons about faith, obedience, and the power of God to work through His faithful servants.

Elijah's ministry begins abruptly with his prophetic announcement of a drought upon the land of Israel, as a consequence of the nation's idolatry and disobedience. Despite his humble origins as a Tishbite from Gilead, Elijah boldly confronts King Ahab and Queen Jezebel, challenging the prevailing culture of idol worship and calling the people to repentance.

Lessons:

One of the primary lessons we can learn from the life of Elijah is the importance of unwavering faith and trust in God, even in the midst of uncertainty and opposition. Throughout his ministry, Elijah demonstrates remarkable faithfulness and dependence on God, seeking His guidance and provision in all circumstances. His courageous confrontations with the prophets of Baal on Mount Carmel, as well as his solitary stand against the forces of evil, serve as powerful examples of faith in action.

Furthermore, Elijah's story underscores the theme of God's sovereignty and providence over human affairs. Through his miraculous interventions, such as the provision of food by ravens, the raising of the widow's son, and the defeat of the prophets of Baal, God demonstrates His power to work through His faithful servant and accomplish His purposes. Elijah's experiences serve as a reminder of God's faithfulness and provision for those who trust in Him wholeheartedly.

Additionally, Elijah's ministry offers lessons about the importance of perseverance and resilience in the face of adversity. Despite facing opposition, persecution, and threats on his life, Elijah remains steadfast in his commitment to God and continues to fulfill his prophetic calling with unwavering determination. His example challenges believers to persevere in their faith, even when confronted with trials and challenges, knowing that God is faithful to sustain and strengthen them through every difficulty.

Moreover, Elijah's encounters with God, such as his experience of the still small voice on Mount Horeb, provide valuable insights into the nature of divine communication and the importance of cultivating intimacy with God through prayer and meditation. Elijah's willingness to listen for God's voice and respond obediently serves as a model for believers seeking to discern God's will and direction for their lives.

In conclusion, the life and ministry of Elijah offer valuable lessons about faith, obedience, and the power of God to work through His faithful servants. Through his unwavering faithfulness, courageous confrontations, and intimate encounters with God, Elijah serves as an inspiration and example for believers of all ages. His story challenges us to trust in God's promises, to remain steadfast in our commitment to Him, and to boldly proclaim His truth in a world desperately in need of His grace and redemption.

Queen Athaliah

Queen Athaliah, a figure prominently featured in the Old Testament, stands as a cautionary tale of the dangers of unchecked ambition, idolatry, and the consequences of forsaking God's commands. Her story, chronicled primarily in 2 Kings and 2 Chronicles, offers valuable lessons about the corrupting influence of power and the importance of remaining faithful to God's principles.

Athaliah was the daughter of King Ahab and Queen Jezebel of Israel, known for their promotion of idol worship and persecution of God's prophets. After marrying Jehoram, the king of Judah, Athaliah sought to extend her influence and secure her family's dynasty by any means necessary. Upon her husband's death, Athaliah seized power and embarked on a ruthless campaign to eliminate any potential rivals to the throne, including her own grandchildren.

Lessons:

One of the primary lessons we can learn from the life of Queen Athaliah is the destructive power of ambition and pride. Driven by her desire for power and control, Athaliah abandoned all moral and ethical considerations, resorting to violence and treachery to achieve her goals. Her ruthless pursuit of power led to the massacre of her own family members and the imposition of idolatry upon the nation of Judah.

Furthermore, Athaliah's reign serves as a vivid example of the consequences of forsaking God's commands and embracing idolatry. Under her rule, the nation of Judah experienced a period of spiritual and moral decay, marked by the worship of false gods and the oppression of God's people. Athaliah's idolatrous practices brought divine judgment upon the nation and resulted in widespread suffering and hardship.

Additionally, Athaliah's story highlights the importance of remaining vigilant against the influence of evil and the need to resist the temptations of power and worldly ambition. Despite her attempts to establish her reign and perpetuate her family's dynasty, Athaliah's rule ultimately proved to be short-lived, as God raised up a young heir, Joash, to overthrow her tyranny and restore true worship to Judah.

Moreover, Athaliah's downfall serves as a reminder of God's faithfulness to His promises and His ability to work through unlikely circumstances to accomplish His purposes. Despite the apparent triumph of evil and the oppression of God's people, God remained sovereign over the affairs of nations and raised up a deliverer to execute justice and bring about restoration.

In conclusion, the life and reign of Queen Athaliah offer valuable lessons about the dangers of unchecked ambition, idolatry, and the consequences of forsaking God's commands. Her story serves as a cautionary tale for believers about the corrupting influence of power and the importance of remaining faithful to God's principles, even in the face of adversity and opposition. Athaliah's legacy challenges us to examine our own hearts and motives, and to seek to honor God in all that we do, trusting in His faithfulness to guide and sustain us through every trial and temptation.